MR. NEW-SCHOOL'S ALPHABET BOOK

By Brian Barber

Mr. New-School

Archway Publishing books may be ordered through booksellers or by contacting:

Archway Publishing
1663 Liberty Drive
Bloomington, IN 47403
www.archwaypublishing.com
844-669-3957

ISBN: 978-1-6657-2072-4 (sc)
ISBN: 978-1-6657-2851-5 (hc)
ISBN: 978-1-6657-2073-1 (e)

Print information available on the last page.

Archway Publishing rev. date: 08/11/2022

Art School

A is for art school.

Arts is cool and you can rap and sing.

You can dance and act and draw anything.

A is for art school.

New-School Fact:
A student who studies art is more likely to be recognized for academic achievement.

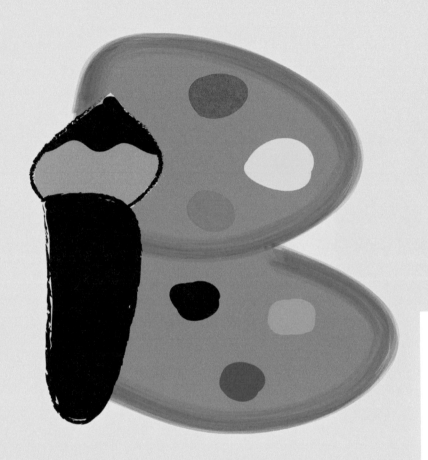

Brush

B is for brush.

The brush is the tool
that you want to use

When you want to paint
a new pair of shoes.

B is for brush.

New-School Fact:
Most paintbrushes are
mechanically produced but
professional artists tend to
use handmade brushes.

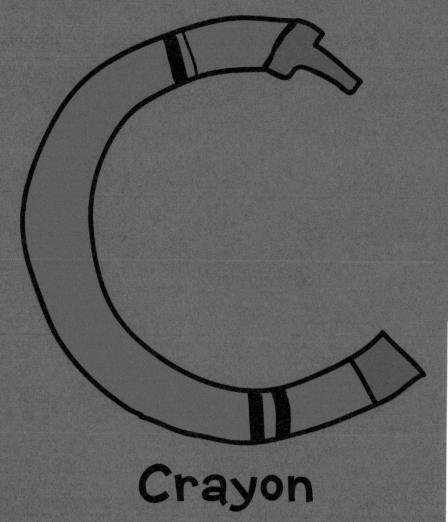

Crayon

C is for crayon.

The crayon is the one
for coloring fun.

Grab a coloring book and
you can color the sun.

C is for crayon.

New-School Fact:
Crayons are made
from paraffin wax
and color pigment.

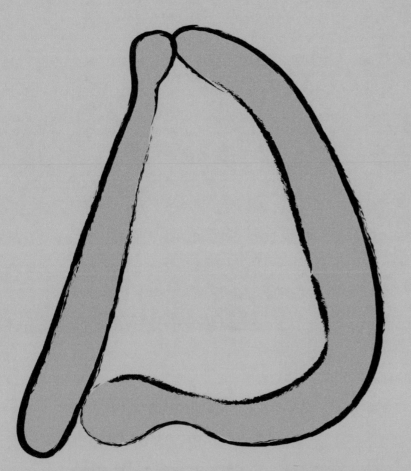

Drumsticks

D is for drumsticks.

Drumsticks can hit and make the drum beat smooth.

I love it when the drummer boy is making me groove.

D is for drumsticks.

New-School Fact: Drumsticks can be made of different woods such as hickory, oak, and maple.

E is for electricity.

Electricity is power that can cause a shock

And it helps the electric guitar to rock.

E is for electricity.

New-School Fact: The electric guitar was invented in the early 1930s.

Electricity

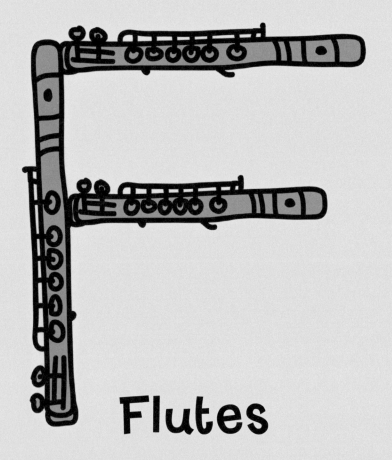

Flutes

F is for flutes.

The flute makes the notes
that sound so nice

And cool and smooth just
like skates and ice.

F is for flutes.

New-School Fact:
Flutes have been around
for thousands of years
and early flutes were
made of animal bones.

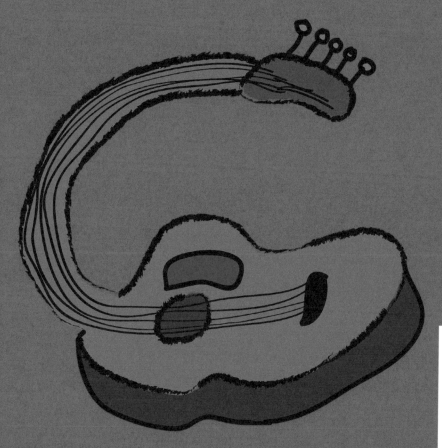

Guitar

G is for guitar.

Guitars are good for you to play and sing.

Get your fingers ready so you can pluck the strings.

G is for guitar.

New-School Fact: Guitars generally have six strings but some guitars can have four, seven, eight, ten, or even twelve strings.

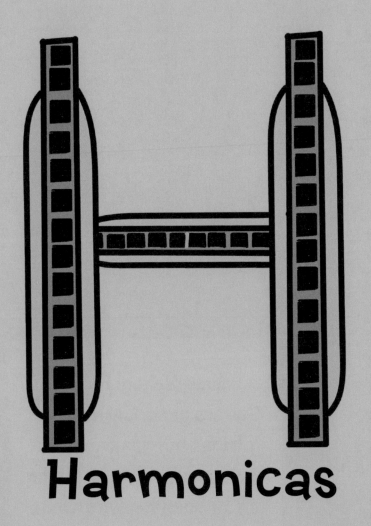

Harmonicas

H is for harmonicas.

Harmonicas are cool
for the 12-bar blues.

You can play them any way
that you feel or choose.

H is for harmonicas.

New-School Fact:
There are three major
types of harmonicas: the
diatonic harmonica, the
chromatic harmonica, and
the tremolo harmonica.

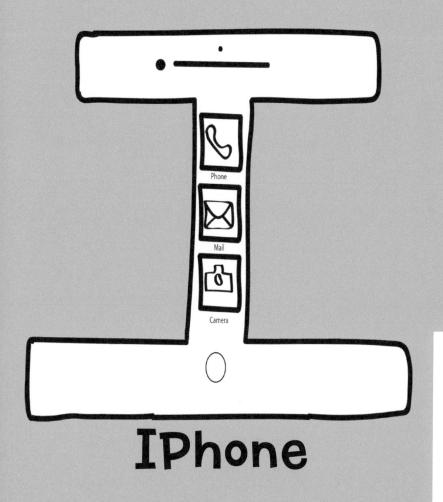

IPhone

I is for IPhone.

The IPhone is technology that's full of apps

And music you can download to dance and clap.

I is for IPhone.

New-School Fact:
The most expensive parts of smartphones are the memory and the screen.

Jazz
Saxophone

J is for the jazz saxophone.

The jazz saxophone is
as cool as can be.

Any band with a saxophone
is groovy to me.

J is for the jazz saxophone.

New-School Fact:
Although the saxophone
is commonly made of
brass, it is classified as a
woodwind instrument.

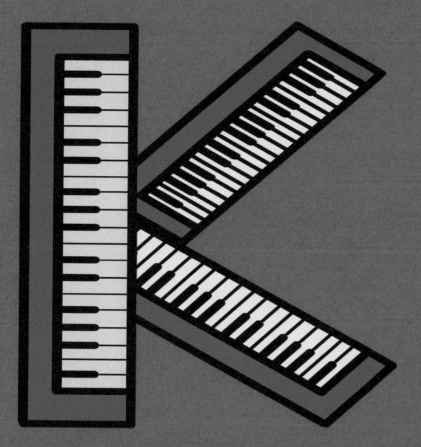

Keyboards

K is for keyboards.

Keyboards make the
sounds when you
press the keys:

Black keys, white keys,
any keys you please.

K is for keyboards.

New-School Fact:
Keyboards are
electronically powered
and capable of producing
a wide range of sounds.

It's
Cool
It's
Cool
It's
Mr.
New-School

Lyrics

L is for lyrics.

Lyrics are the words
that we sing or rap.

They make your head start
to nod and your fingers snap.

L is for lyrics.

New-School Fact:
Although lyrics are commonly
thought to be the words of a
musical composition; a lyric is
also a type of poem in which a
poet expresses strong emotion.

Music

M is for music.

Music is the sounds
that we love to hear,

January to December,
any time of the year.

M is for music.

New-School Fact:
Few activities are
connected with using
the entire brain; music
is one of them.

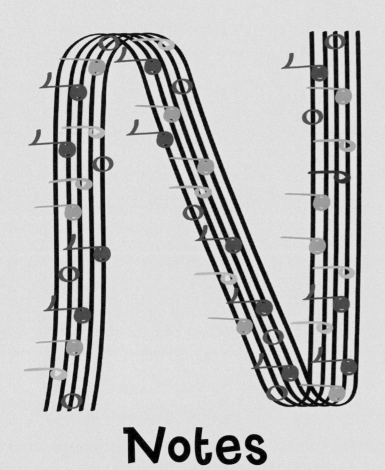

Notes

N is for notes.

Notes are the symbols that sit on the staff.

You have whole notes, quarter notes, and even halfs.

N is for notes.

New-School Fact: Musical notes represent two things: the duration and the pitch of a sound.

O is for old-school records.

Old-school records used to play when party people used to boogie way back in the day.

O is for old-school records.

New-School Fact: Records are made out of a material called vinyl and are played on a device called a record player.

Old-School Records

Paint

P is for paint.

Paint makes pictures look vivid and colorful.

Hang a painting on the wall and make the room look wonderful.

P is for paint.

New-School Fact: Paint colors can impact a person's mood and influence any type of emotion.

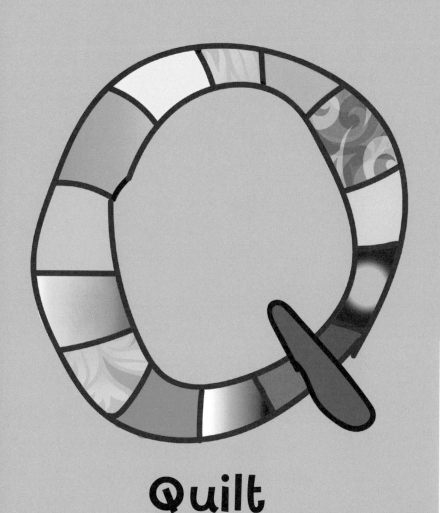

Quilt

Q is for quilt.

A quilt keeps you warm
in the bed at night.

It's made of fabric
and stitches and lots
of colors, alright.

Q is for quilt.

New-School Fact:
Quilts are usually
decorative in design and
are made by stitching
layers of fabric together.

Recess

R is for recess.

Recess is the time in
the middle of the day
where kids run, jump,
and have fun and play.

R is for recess.

New-School Fact:
Recess is a great activity for
reducing stress, exercising,
and developing social skills.

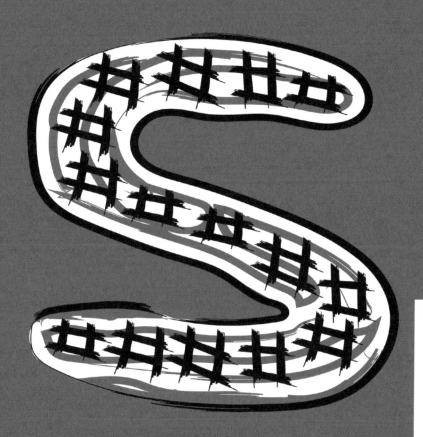

Sharps

S is for sharps.

Sharps raise the
pitch of a note a bit

So when you play the
tones, it is a perfect fit.

S is for sharps.

New-School Fact:
A sharp is categorized
as an accidental in
musical notation.
A sharp makes a pitch
slightly higher.

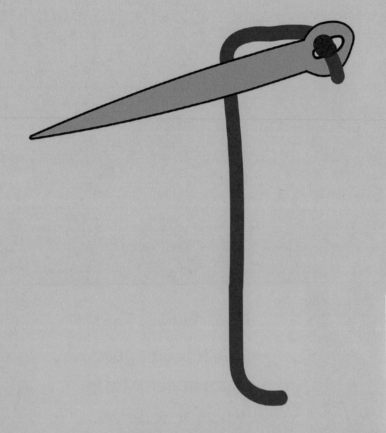

Thread

T is for thread.

Thread is what is used when
you're sewing clothes

And creating new styles
for the fashion shows.

T is for thread.

New-School Fact:
Thread can be made from
different materials including
silk, cotton, and polyester.

Unison

U is for unison.

Unison is when we sing all together as one,

The same time, unified equals so much fun.

U is for unison.

New-School Fact:
The meaning of unison is literally "one sound."

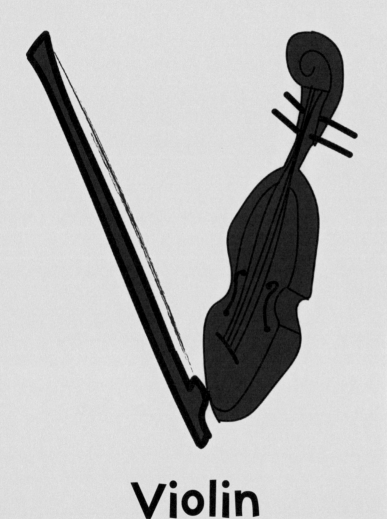

Violin

V is for violin.

The violin is a string instrument, you know.

With four strings, it sings when you use a bow.

V is for violin.

New-School Fact:
Violins are made up of many parts including the body, strings, neck and fingerboard, pegbox, tailpiece, chin rest, bridge, f-holes, and scroll.

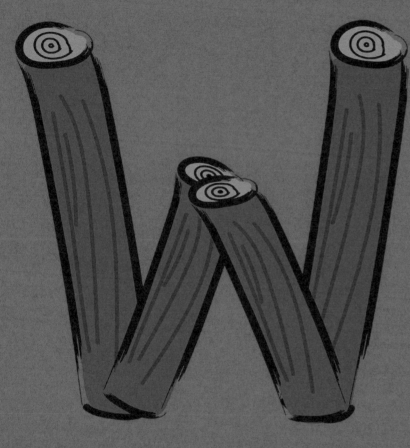

W is for wood.

Wood is good for you
to sand and shape

When you have a sculpture
that you want to make.

W is for wood.

Wood

New-School Fact:
The four main wood
carving styles are
whittling, relief carving,
carving in the round,
and chip carving.

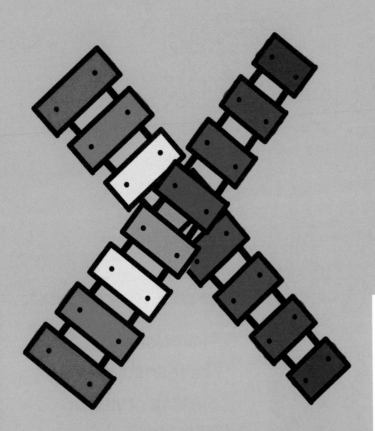

X is for xylophones.

Xylophones are percussion
instruments you hit

With mallets that make
the sound too legit.

X is for xylophones.

Xylophones

New-School Fact:
The xylophone belongs to a
percussion family group called
"pitch percussion" since it
can play different tones.

Yeah!!!

Y is for yeah!!!

Yeah!!! is the sound
that we all make

When we're having
so much fun that
we cannot fake.

Y is for yeah!!!

New-School Fact:
Mr. New-School loves
to make the crowd
say YEAH!!!

Zigzag

Z is for zigzag.

A zigzag is a line that turns left and right.

You can draw as many zigzags as you like.

Z is for zigzag.

New-School Fact:
The zigzag pattern is often seen in fashion, artwork, and architecture.

Dear Parents/Guardians and Educators,

The Mr. New-School Font is a typeface based on the animated educational character, Mr. New-School. Every symbol was crafted, hand-sketched, and traced with a digital brush tool. Each letter has its own identity as it represents an individual aspect of arts and education. The use of vibrant colors and distinct brush strokes makes the Mr. New-School Font appealing to children and adults alike. The font is used in conjunction with the Mr. New-School Curriculum.

Sincerely,
Mr. New-School

Printed in the United States
by Baker & Taylor Publisher Services